Contents

Vocabulary

dangerous   extinguishers
daredevil   gymnastics
equipment   injury
Evel Knievel   performer

1. FILM STUNTS

Stunt performers are the daredevils of the film and TV world.

Whenever a TV or film script needs someone to leap from a burning building or fall down stairs, a stuntman or woman will usually perform the stunt instead of the actor.

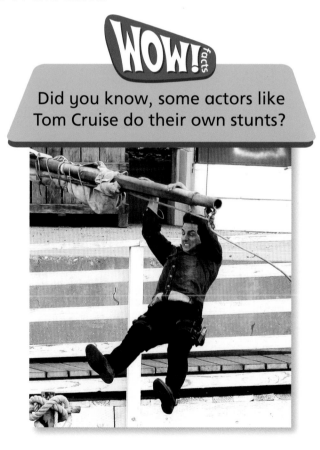

WOW! facts

Did you know, some actors like Tom Cruise do their own stunts?

Some daredevils work as stunt doubles.

They must be good stunt performers and, with the help of clothes and wigs, look like the actor they are 'doubling' for.

Vic Armstrong

Vic Armstrong is the world's most famous stunt double.

In his career, he has doubled for many famous people, including for actors playing James Bond, Superman and Indiana Jones.

Which is which? Vic Armstrong doubles as Indiana Jones.

Vic Armstrong looked so much like Harrison Ford, who played Indiana Jones, that crew members on the film set often mistook him for Ford.

Stunt performers need lots of different skills for the different types of stunt they perform.

Type of stunt	Useful skills
falling	gymnastics or trampolining
fighting	boxing or martial arts
riding	horse or motorbike riding
driving	driving cars or trucks at speed
water	swimming or scuba diving

Some performers specialise in one type of stunt.

Russ Swift is a specialist stunt driver. He has performed his stunts both in live shows and on TV.

2. LIVE STUNTS

Some stuntmen and women perform live stunts for an audience.

These daredevils include escape artists, wire walkers, free climbers and stunt drivers.

The Knievels

Evel Knievel and his son Robbie are famous for their daredevil motorbike stunts.

They have jumped over:
- 13 buses and trucks
- 17 cars
- wide canyons

Evel Knievel is also famous for holding the world record for the most broken bones in a lifetime. He has broken 433 bones!

Man on a wire

High-wire artist Nik Wallenda is famous for his high-wire performances without a safety net.

Widely known as 'The King of the Wire', he holds many world records and, in 2012, was the first person to walk a tightrope directly over Niagara Falls.

In a spin

Escape artist Rick Maisel performed a very dangerous stunt.

He got into a washing machine wearing six pairs of handcuffs and two pairs of leg irons.

Then the washing machine was turned on!

The human spider

Daredevil Alain Robert likes climbing tall buildings.

He climbs skyscrapers without a safety rope or any climbing equipment.

No wonder he is called 'The Human Spider'!

3. SOME OF THE BEST FILM STUNTS

Bond bungee

In the film *Goldeneye*, James Bond dives 220 metres off a dam!

This amazing stunt was performed by the British stuntman Wayne Michaels.

It was filmed in one take. At the time, it was the highest bungee jump in history!

Scary slide

The actor Jackie Chan did all his own stunts. He did not use a stunt double.

One of his most famous stunts was sliding down the side of this 21-storey building – *without a safety harness!*

Hanging on!

Zoe Bell won an award for her amazing film stunt.

Somehow, she hung onto the bonnet of a car travelling at 85 miles per hour, while another car tried to force it off the road!

Fantastic free fall

Stuntman Dar Robinson made a record-breaking fall from a window for the movie *Sharky's Machine.*

In one of the most dangerous stunts ever filmed, Dar fell over 70 metres *without a safety wire!* That's the height of nearly 16 double decker buses!

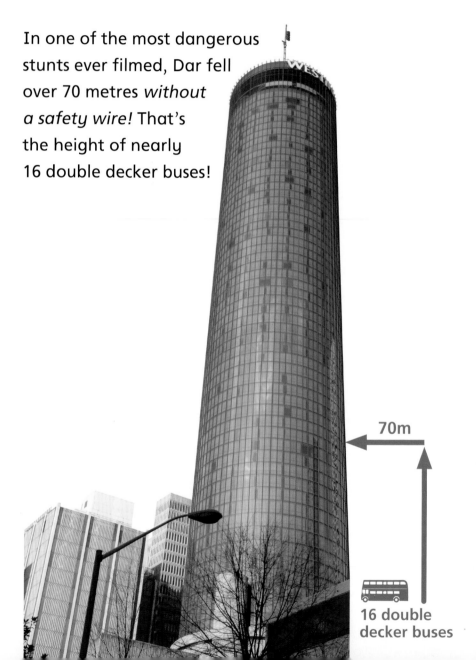

70m

16 double decker buses

The incredible flip

In *The Dark Knight*, an 18-wheel truck is flipped onto its back!

To do this amazing flip, a huge air ram pushed the back end of the lorry 15 metres into the air!

4. STUNT SAFETY

There are three parts to every stunt:
- planning
- practising
- performing

A stunt has to be *planned* so it is safe.

Stunt performers are brave but they are not stupid! They do not take unnecessary risks.

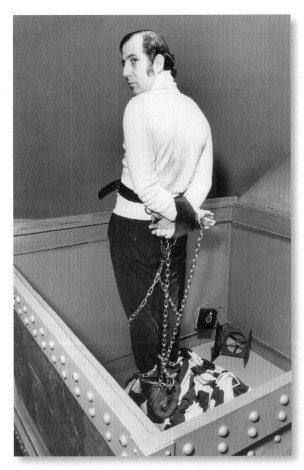

The stunt is *practised* until they are sure it can be done safely – things like wires and crash mats are also used for protection.

Only then is the stunt *performed*.

Fire safety

Fire stunts are especially dangerous.

Stuntmen and women wear fireproof clothing to protect themselves.

They also cover their skin and hair with a special gel.

But things can still go wrong, so medical help and fire extinguishers are always on set.

WOW! facts

Stunt performers hold their breath while doing fire stunts. If they don't, they could burn their lungs.

Glass safety

Jumping through glass is very dangerous but stunt performers use rubber glass. It looks and breaks like glass – but feels soft like rubber!

Falling safely

Falling from a great height could be fatal. So stunt performers learn how to fall and land safely. Giant air bags are used to land on.

WOW! facts

Stuntman Martin Shenton holds the world record for falling down the most stairs – he fell down 109 of them!

5. SO YOU WANT TO BE A STUNT PERFORMER?

Q: Would you like to spend your days being set on fire, thrown out of windows and crashing cars?

If the answer is yes, you might like to think about becoming a stunt performer.

Q: What sorts of people make good stunt performers?

A: People who are:
- physically fit
- good at a wide range of sports
- able to work as part of a team

Q: How old must I be?
A: At least 18 years old.

Q: What qualifications do I need?
A: You will need to show you can perform at least six different sports and skills, such as boxing, diving, horse riding, gymnastics, driving and swimming.

Q: Anything else?

A: You will need to have worked as a film or TV actor or extra for at least 60 days.

Q: So is being a stunt performer the job for you?

You decide!

For the job	Against the job
being physically active	long hours on set
being in films and on TV	not always easy to find work
doing a variety of exciting work	danger of injury
travelling to different places	spending time away from your family

Questions

Name an actor who performs their own stunts. *(page 5)*

What type of skills do you need if you are going to perform a water stunt? *(page 8)*

What kind of things did the Knievels jump over? *(page 10)*

Why is Alain Robert called 'The Human Spider'? *(page 14)*

What world record does Martin Shenton hold? *(page 25)*

How old do you need to be before you can become a stunt performer? *(page 28)*

INDEX